Original title:
Snug by the Snow-Filled Sky

Copyright © 2024 Creative Arts Management OÜ
All rights reserved.

Author: Amelia Montgomery
ISBN HARDBACK: 978-9916-94-410-3
ISBN PAPERBACK: 978-9916-94-411-0

Melodies of the Snowy Whisper

Whispers dance on frosty air,
Soft flakes fall without a care.
Each one tells a silent tale,
Wrapped in winter's gentle veil.

Branches bend with purest white,
Moonlight bathes the world in light.
Nature breathes in quiet grace,
Magic lives in every space.

Embracing the Icicle Sparkle

Icicles hang like crystal dreams,
Glistening bright in sunlit beams.
They catch the light, a dazzling show,
Nature's gems in forms that glow.

The chill of air, a gentle bite,
Hearts grow warm, spirits in flight.
As frosty sighs swirl all around,
In this beauty, peace is found.

Laid Back in Winter's Peace

Sitting still, the world at rest,
In this calm, I feel so blessed.
Snowflakes drift, a soft embrace,
Time slows down, a gentle pace.

Hot cocoa warms my cozy soul,
As winter's magic takes its toll.
With every breath, a silent cheer,
In winter's peace, I hold you near.

Gathered Close in the Frozen Glow

Around the fire, laughter bright,
Fingers warm in shining light.
Families gather, stories share,
In the glow of love, we care.

The crispness hugs us, tight and bold,
Creating bonds, new and old.
Wrapped in warmth, our hearts ignite,
Together, facing winter's bite.

The Comfort of Cold Stillness

In the silent night, whispers flow,
Echoes of dreams in the moon's soft glow.
Each breath is a frost, crisp and bright,
A blanket of peace under starry light.

Frozen branches sway, shadows dance,
Nature's quietude holds a trance.
The world sleeps deep, wrapped in white,
Finding solace in the cold, still night.

Tales Told in the Winter's Chill

Stories flicker in the fire's warm hold,
Of ancient times, in the winter's cold.
Wisps of smoke drift, weaving a tale,
Of lovers and journeys, both frail and frail.

The wind carries secrets, a haunting tune,
As frost grips the earth beneath the moon.
Whispers of laughter, ghosts of the past,
Seeking the warmth that may never last.

Nights Drenched in Moonlit White

Beneath the glow of a silver sphere,
The world transforms, so crystal clear.
Snowflakes twirl in a dancing ballet,
Painting the night in the softest way.

Silence envelopes, a calming embrace,
Footsteps linger, a delicate trace.
Stars twinkle softly, like diamonds bright,
In nights so tranquil, drenched in white.

Where Winter's Heart Beats Softly

In the heart of winter, a pulse unseen,
Nature lies still in a tranquil sheen.
Whispers of life beneath the snow,
Waiting for spring to unfurl and grow.

Frozen rivers hold secrets deep,
While shadows of night begin to creep.
The quiet hum of life persists,
In the soft lullaby, winter exists.

Midnight Mirth Under a Blanket of Snow

In the hush of night, stars glow bright,
Snowflakes dance, a pure delight.
Whispers of joy in the frosty air,
Children laugh without a care.

Footprints trace where dreams have flown,
Underneath the moonlight's throne.
Magic swirls in the chilly breeze,
Midnight mirth puts hearts at ease.

Gentle Lullabies of the Winter Winds

Winds carry whispers through the trees,
Softly humming like gentle seas.
Each note blankets the earth in sleep,
Winter's watch over dreams we keep.

Icicles glisten, a crystal song,
Nature's melody, sweet and strong.
As night falls, the world grows still,
Lullabies echo, a tender thrill.

Celestial Hues Over Frozen Fields

Dawn paints the sky in shades of gray,
Beneath the frost, the shadows play.
Golden rays pierce the winter chill,
Fields sparkle with a flurry at will.

Celestial hues dance, bright and bold,
Stories of warmth through the cold unfold.
A tapestry woven with hope anew,
As life stirs slowly in morning's view.

A Soft Embrace of Winter's Breath

Breath of winter wraps the land tight,
Soft as wool, it embraces the night.
Frost-kissed branches, a delicate sight,
Nature rests under a silvery light.

The world whispers secrets, quiet and bright,
In this stillness, everything feels right.
A treasure to hold, a moment to keep,
In winter's breath, we drift into sleep.

Adventures in a Frosty Wonderland

In a land where snowflakes dance,
Children laugh and take a chance.
Sleds are flying, joy takes flight,
In the frost, hearts feel so light.

Icicles shimmer in the sun,
Chasing fun is just begun.
Snowmen stand with carrot nose,
In this place where wonder grows.

Whispers of the winter breeze,
Rustle through the frozen trees.
Hot cocoa warms our chilly hands,
As we play in these white lands.

Time stands still in this delight,
Underneath the moon's soft light.
Every moment's filled with cheer,
Frosty wonder, precious year.

The Night of Stars and Soft Snow

Beneath a sky of twinkling light,
The world transforms in hush of night.
Soft snow blankets every sound,
As magic drapes the earth around.

Footsteps crunch on paths so bright,
Guided by the stars' pure light.
Whispers of the winter's song,
In this place, where dreams belong.

Fires crackle, warmth and glow,
Through the windows, smiles show.
In the silence, hearts connect,
In the night, we feel respect.

Sleepy towns wrapped in peace,
Worries fade, tensions cease.
As the snowflakes gently fall,
We discover love, our all.

Through the Glare of Snowy Twilight

In twilight's glow, the snowflakes dance,
A gentle hush, a fleeting chance.
The world transformed, a pearl-white sea,
Where dreams take flight, wild and free.

Beneath the sky's soft, dim embrace,
The silver whispers, a calmest space.
Footprints left in winter's breath,
Each telling tales, of beauty's depth.

Shadows Beneath the Frosted Canopy

Tall trees stand, in quiet grace,
Their branches wrapped in winter's lace.
Shadows linger, soft and deep,
Where secrets lie, the cold winds sweep.

Beneath the frost, the earth holds still,
A world asleep, by winter's will.
Yet underneath, the heart beats true,
Waiting for spring to break on through.

A Glow Within the Wintry Realm

Inside the hearth, a glowing light,
Banishes the chill of night.
With every flicker, warmth will rise,
In whispered tales of starry skies.

Through frosted windows, dreams ignite,
In cozy nooks, the heart feels right.
A gentle glow, a tender sigh,
As winter sings its lullaby.

When Silence Wraps the Evening

When silence wraps the mountains high,
A quietude beneath the sky.
The world hushed, in stillness profound,
Where only hope and peace are found.

As stars appear, like gems in dark,
The night enchants with soothing spark.
In the calm, our worries cease,
Embraced by night, we find our peace.

The Lull of Snow-Blanketed Nights

The world lies hushed beneath the white,
Stars twinkle gently, shining bright.
Blankets of snow, soft and deep,
Cradle the earth, as night drifts to sleep.

Trees stand silent, a frozen choir,
A soft wind carries whispers higher.
Footprints vanish, erasing the past,
In this serene moment, time seems to last.

Moonlight dances on the glimmering frost,
In this winter beauty, we find the lost.
Nature's lullaby, sweet and low,
Inviting dreams in the silent glow.

Rest now, beneath the starry sheen,
In this stillness, magic can be seen.
The lull of snow, a tender embrace,
Wraps the world in its gentle grace.

Cuddled in a Cold Embrace

Wrapped in layers, cozy and warm,
The chilly air holds a curious charm.
Under the blankets, we snuggle tight,
While the world outside sparkles in white.

Hot cocoa sips, laughter and cheer,
In this cold embrace, love draws near.
Frosted windows, a misty glaze,
Inside we bask in the fire's blaze.

Snowflakes dance in the moonlit glow,
A soft kiss of winter, enchanting show.
Hands intertwine, hearts softly race,
Cuddled together in this cold embrace.

With each soft flake that gently falls,
We hear the winter's tranquil calls.
Wrapped in warmth, we hold on tight,
Together, we shine in the still of the night.

While the Sky Falls Softly

While the sky falls softly, watch and see,
Gentle flakes flutter, wild and free.
Each one a secret, a story to tell,
In their quiet descent, they weave a spell.

The earth receives this winter's gift,
As cold winds sigh and shadows drift.
Kissing the ground, they sprinkle white,
Transforming the world into a dreamlike sight.

Families gather, building cheer,
Snowmen arise as laughter draws near.
In this magical moment, time slows down,
While the sky falls softly, nature's gown.

So let us cherish these fleeting days,
As winter's beauty wraps us in its ways.
While the sky weeps joy, we stand in bliss,
Embracing the peace in every snow-kissed kiss.

Frost-Covered Whispers

Frost-covered whispers dance on the breeze,
Soft and fleeting, like whispers of trees.
Each blade of grass dons a crystal crown,
As the world transforms, wearing its gown.

In the quiet morn, the sun breaks through,
Painting the landscape with glimmers anew.
Each crystal sparkles, a moment's grace,
Caught in the glow of winter's embrace.

Voices drift little through the chilly air,
Carried on winds with a tender care.
Frosted branches sway, a soft ballet,
As nature breathes life into a cold day.

So listen closely to winter's tune,
In the heart of the night or the glimmer of noon.
Frost-covered whispers, soft and clear,
Guide us through winter, holding us near.

Stories Shared in Icy Silence

In the hush of winter's breath,
Whispers float on frosty air,
Tales of warmth, of love and death,
Echo softly, everywhere.

Fires crackle, shadows dance,
Old souls gather, hearts entwined,
Memories spark with each glance,
Frozen moments, pure and kind.

Under stars, in silver light,
Voices soft, yet full of might,
In this calm, we find our way,
Bonded stories here to stay.

So let the silence wrap us tight,
In icy stillness, hearts ignite,
Shared in warmth, we break the chill,
Together, time stands always still.

Beneath the Cloak of Falling Snow

Snowflakes swirl, a gentle sigh,
Covering earth like a quilt,
Nature whispers, soft goodbye,
In this beauty, peace is built.

Branches bend with frosty lace,
Each step muffled, world asleep,
In this stillness, find your place,
Secrets of the night we keep.

Crimson firelight from afar,
Guides the wanderers' retreat,
Underneath the evening star,
Finding warmth in hearts that meet.

Cloaked in dreams, let spirits soar,
Beneath the snow, we seek for more,
Magic weaves in quiet night,
Hearts united, pure delight.

A Sanctuary in Winter's Heart

Within the cold, a refuge found,
Whispers warm in frosty air,
Candlelight in shadows bound,
Embers dance without a care.

Thick blankets wrap us tight,
Holding stories, joys, and fears,
In this haven, soft delight,
We carve our dreams, erase our tears.

Outside, the world in silence drapes,
While laughter floats like drifting snow,
In this space, our truth escapes,
Together, we let worries go.

In winter's heart, we find our way,
Sanctuary built in love's array,
Where all is gentle, safe, and bright,
A lasting bond in winter's night.

The Shimmer of Quiet Nights

Moonlight spills like liquid grace,
On the snow, a silver sheen,
In this calm, we find our place,
Peaceful moments, softly keen.

Stars twinkle in velvet skies,
Whispers travel on the breeze,
Night's embrace, a sweet surprise,
Gentle thoughts, like dancing leaves.

Every breath, a whispered prayer,
In the stillness, hearts align,
Cocooned in warmth that we share,
Wrapped in love, we intertwine.

The shimmer of these quiet nights,
Fills our souls with pure delights,
In the dark, we chase the light,
Together, we embrace the night.

The Kindness of a Winter's Night

The stars above shine bright,
Whispers of the cold delight.
A blanket soft, the snowflakes fall,
Wrapping the world in a gentle thrall.

Footprints trace a silent path,
Amidst the quiet, nature's math.
The moon's glow, a silver guide,
In winter's chill, our hearts abide.

Frosty Fingertips on Glass

Frosty patterns, delicate lace,
On windows, nature's embrace.
With every breath, the world exhales,
Stories hidden in icy trails.

The dawn awakes in hues so bright,
Painting the morning with pure light.
Each moment still, a pause in time,
In this season, a silent rhyme.

The Enchantment of Brisk Breezes

Brisk breezes dance through the trees,
Carrying whispers, secrets tease.
Leaves tremble in the frosty air,
Nature's music, beyond compare.

A chill that sparks the fire's glow,
Comfort found in warmth's soft flow.
In every breath, a crisp delight,
The enchantment of the winter night.

Winter's Breath on Whispers

Winter's breath, a gentle sigh,
Echoes softly, to the sky.
Frost-kissed air where silence reigns,
A world transformed, where beauty gains.

In hush of night, the moon's embrace,
Illuminates the tranquil space.
Whispers float on icy streams,
In winter's fold, we find our dreams.

The Art of Winter's Stillness

Stillness blankets the world so wide,
Silent whispers where shadows hide.
Trees adorned in white, they sway,
Nature sleeps, tucked soft away.

Footprints crunch on a frozen ground,
Magic woven in silence found.
Each breath hangs in frosty air,
Winter's grace, beyond compare.

Brittle branches bow with snow,
An artful dance, a gentle flow.
In the quiet, beauty thrives,
Winter's peace truly arrives.

Time slows down in this sacred space,
A moment held in nature's embrace.
In stillness, we find solace true,
The art of winter, a love anew.

Beneath a Canopy of Frost

Beneath a canopy, white and bright,
Frosty leaves catch the morning light.
Each blade of grass, a crystal prize,
Nature's jewels before our eyes.

The world transforms with every dawn,
A silver quilt, pristine and drawn.
Branches shimmer as they greet,
Winter's breath, both sharp and sweet.

Whispers travel on icy air,
Songs of winter, soft and rare.
Within this realm, our spirits soar,
Frosty magic forevermore.

Beneath the hush of frosty skies,
Hope awakens, never dies.
In every flake, a story spun,
Under frost, we become one.

Warmth in a Winter's Kiss

A winter's kiss upon my cheek,
Soft as dreams, yet bold and sleek.
Snowflakes dance, a swirling bliss,
In this chill, I find my miss.

Hands entwined, hearts beat as one,
In the cold, our warmth has spun.
Laughter echoes through the night,
Love's embrace, a guiding light.

Together we brave the icy air,
Wrapped in whispers, a tender care.
In this season, hope renews,
Winter's kiss, a love that stews.

Through frosted panes, we watch the stars,
Dreaming dreams that travel far.
In the hush, our spirits rise,
Warmth ignites beneath cold skies.

The Glint of Stars on Snow

The glint of stars on blankets white,
Twinkling gently through the night.
Snowflakes shimmer as they fall,
Nature's magic, a wondrous call.

Underneath the vast expanse,
Dreamers gather, lost in chance.
Each breath mingles with the cold,
Stories whispered, legends told.

Footsteps echo in the snow,
A quiet path where soft winds blow.
In the stillness, dreams take flight,
Guided by starlit light.

As shadows stretch and time does pause,
The world reflects with perfect cause.
In winter's heart, we find our way,
Stars on snow, where hopes will stay.

A Shield from Winter's Bite

The wind howls fierce, a chilling breeze,
Yet in our hearts, we find our ease.
A warm embrace, a steadfast hold,
Together we stand, brave and bold.

The world outside is white and cold,
But in our nook, we share our gold.
With blankets thick and laughter light,
We find our warmth, a pure delight.

The fire crackles, sparks dance high,
While shadows play upon the sky.
In winter's grip, we're snug and tight,
Our love, the shield from winter's bite.

Together Under the Frosty Spell

Beneath the stars, the world is still,
Wrapped in blankets, time does fill.
The frosty air, a gentle sigh,
Together here, just you and I.

The snowflakes fall, a quiet dance,
In every drift, we find romance.
With whispered dreams, we softly dwell,
Together wrapped in winter's spell.

Our laughter rings, a melody,
In frosty fields, we're wild and free.
Hand in hand, we roam and swell,
Forever lost in this sweet spell.

The Soft Light of Midnight Snow

The midnight hour, a hush descends,
As soft light glows, the silence lends.
Each flake a whisper, pure and bright,
Transforming all beneath the night.

In moonlit glades, the world aglow,
A quiet wonder, deep and slow.
With every breath, the magic flows,
In this stillness, our love grows.

We dance beneath the silver sheen,
A waltz of dreams, serene and clean.
In this embrace, we're lost, we know,
Together here in midnight snow.

Wrapped in Frost and Glow

The morning breaks, a crystal sight,
Wrapped in frost, the world is bright.
The sun peeks through, a gentle warm,
Embracing all, a tender charm.

With every step, the crunching sound,
A symphony of winter found.
We wander close, hearts all aglow,
In every breath, the magic flows.

Together we pause, the world at rest,
In this moment, we are blessed.
Wrapped in frost and glow so fine,
Forever in love, you're mine.

Hearth's Glow Against the Night

The fire crackles low and bright,
In shadows that dance with delight.
Warmth envelops the chilly air,
A haven found, a soul laid bare.

Outside the world in silence sleeps,
A blanket of stars, the sky it keeps.
Yet here within this gentle light,
We gather close, hearts shining bright.

Dreaming in a Snow-Kissed World

Soft flakes swirl like whispered dreams,
A canvas white where sunlight beams.
Each breath a cloud, so pure, so light,
In this cold world, all feels right.

Footsteps crunch on frozen ground,
In quiet corners, peace is found.
As twilight falls, the stars ignite,
In this snowy realm of night.

Frosted Branches and Flickering Lights

Beneath the moon, the branches gleam,
With frosted blooms that softly beam.
Twinkling lights like stories tell,
Of winter nights where laughter fell.

The air is crisp, a joyful sound,
As shadows dance upon the ground.
With every flicker, hearts take flight,
Wrapped in magic, pure delight.

Wrapped in Nature's Quietude

In the forest, time moves slow,
A tranquil path where soft winds blow.
With every leaf that gently falls,
Nature whispers, her beauty calls.

The brook hums tunes of peace and calm,
Each note a soothing, healing balm.
Here in stillness, we find our place,
Embraced in nature's warm embrace.

Cozy Whispers in Winter's Embrace

Snowflakes dance upon the breeze,
Cloaked in white, the world at ease.
Chimneys puff their gentle sighs,
As warmth within the hearth replies.

Hot chocolate swirls in mugs so bright,
While laughter lingers through the night.
Blankets piled, a nest of cheer,
In winter's hold, we draw you near.

Outside, the stars are cold and clear,
Yet here, your heart is safe, sincere.
With every whisper, dreams take flight,
In cozy shadows, hearts ignite.

Frosted Dreams Beneath a Blanket of Stars

Beneath the vast and twinkling sky,
Frosted dreams are whispering high.
The moon spills silver on the ground,
In this stillness, peace is found.

Pine trees wrap in icy lace,
As night unfolds its quiet grace.
Each breath a cloud in chilly air,
The world hushed soft, a tranquil prayer.

In the silence, secrets gleam,
Nature holds us in a dream.
Stars above, they shine so bright,
Guiding hearts through tranquil night.

The Hearth's Warm Glow

Crackling flames in cozy nooks,
Shadowed corners, open books.
The glow of embers, soft and red,
Whispers tales of peace instead.

Family gathers, stories shared,
In the warmth, all souls are bared.
Echoes of laughter fill the space,
In the hearth's embrace, we find grace.

Outside the chill may bite and sting,
Yet here, the heart begins to sing.
With every flicker of the flame,
We find our comfort, love the same.

Silence Wrapped in Winter's Quilt

A blanket white drapes over all,
In gentle hush, we hear the call.
Footprints trace a path so light,
In winter's quilt, the world feels right.

Branches bow with laden snow,
In this stillness, time moves slow.
Soft whispers carried on the air,
Nature's secrets linger there.

The quiet hum of life retreats,
Underneath the snow, it beats.
Wrapped in silence, we take a breath,
Winter's beauty conquers death.

Echoes of a Frozen Breath

Whispers trace the icy air,
Softly curling, unaware.
Silent tales of winter's chill,
Time suspended, calm and still.

Fragrant dreams of pine and snow,
Nature's art in gentle flow.
Footsteps linger, echoes fade,
Memories in frost are laid.

In the hush, a crystal gleam,
Captured light, a fragile dream.
Beneath the stars, the world feels right,
Echoes linger in the night.

Every breath a frozen sigh,
Underneath the cosmic sky.
The beauty of this frosty time,
An echo of a whispered rhyme.

Cozy Corners of a Winter's Night

By the fire, a soft glow,
Shadows dance, gently slow.
A cup of warmth held tight,
In cozy corners, pure delight.

Blankets wrapped, stories shared,
Laughter echoes, love declared.
The wind may howl, the snow may drift,
But in our hearts, a soothing gift.

Outside, the world wears white,
But inside, hearts burn bright.
With every moment, time stands still,
In cozy corners, we find our thrill.

Candles flicker, softly sway,
Guiding dreams along the way.
In winter's embrace, we hold on tight,
To all the joys of a winter's night.

The Dance of the Snowfall

Snowflakes twirl, a graceful spin,
Nature's waltz, where dreams begin.
Each flake unique, a story spun,
In the quiet, they softly run.

Joyful laughter fills the air,
Children playing without a care.
Building castles, shaped with glee,
In the dance where hearts run free.

Underneath the silver moon,
Whispers of winter's gentle tune.
As snowy sheets embrace the ground,
In this dance, a peace is found.

When morning breaks, the world aglow,
A dazzling quilt where cold winds blow.
With every flurry, life feels whole,
In the dance of the snowfall's soul.

Glistening Moments of Serenity

A quiet dawn, the world agleam,
Frosty crystals, a brilliant dream.
Nature breathes in whispered light,
Glistening moments, pure delight.

Silent woods in purest peace,
Every worry finds release.
A tranquil heart, a mindful gaze,
In serene spots, our spirits blaze.

The sun peeks through the pines so tall,
Casting jewels that gently fall.
Each glistening orb, a memory made,
In peaceful moments, where dreams cascade.

As twilight falls, the stars align,
Nature holds our hearts, divine.
In these moments, we find our way,
Glistening peace, come what may.

Stars Gathered Around a Fire's Heart

In the hush of night, they gleam bright,
Whispers of warmth in soft twilight,
Flickers dance in shadows deep,
While the world around drifts to sleep.

Embers glow with tales untold,
In flickering light, stories unfold.
Stars twinkle their ancient lore,
Gathered together, forever more.

The fire crackles, a rhythmic sound,
Binding the night with magic profound.
Each spark a wish, a dream to share,
In this circle, we lay our cares bare.

As the night shrinks to dawn's embrace,
The stars fade with a whispered grace.
Yet the warmth lingers, hearts entwined,
In a cosmic bond, eternally aligned.

Frost-Kissed Serenity

Morning light, a gentle glow,
Frost-edged leaves, in a soft bow.
Nature breathes in silence pure,
Wrapped in beauty, a calming cure.

Whispers of cold, a soft caress,
Each crystal spark, nature's finesse.
Trees stand tall in coats of white,
Guardians of secrets, lost in night.

Footsteps crunch on icy ground,
In this serene, enchanted round.
Every breath, a cloud of dreams,
Frost-kissed moments, peace redeems.

As the sun rises, warmth unfurls,
Melting the frost, revealing pearls.
With every ray, joy reappears,
In frost-kissed serenity, calm endears.

Winter's Tapestry of Dreams

Threads of white weave through the trees,
A tapestry sways in winter's breeze.
Each flake, a story, a moment caught,
In the arms of silence, dreams are wrought.

Fires crackle, shadows play,
In the heart of night, we find our way.
Holding tightly to warmth and light,
As the world outside glistens in white.

Whispers of hope in the winter air,
Every breath shared, a lover's prayer.
In the stillness, our dreams take flight,
Embraced in the magic of the soft night.

With every dawn, a promise anew,
Winter's embrace, a healing hue.
Stitched together in love's great seam,
We journey onward, wrapped in dream.

Wrapped in the Silence of White

Snowflakes fall like whispered sighs,
Covering earth where beauty lies.
Wrapped in silence, soft and deep,
In winter's arms, we dream and sleep.

The world transforms, a canvas bright,
Blanketed in peaceful, pure white.
Every tree, each shadowed nook,
Holds a secret, like a book.

Footprints mark the path we tread,
In this snowy realm, we're gently led.
Nature hushes, a lullaby,
Underneath the vast, open sky.

Wrapped in the stillness, hearts unite,
Finding solace in the gentle night.
As the stars twinkle, softly ignite,
Together we stand, in the silence of white.

A Tapestry of Soft Hues

Morning light breaks through the mist,
Soft hues dance in gentle streams,
Whispers of pastel in the air,
A painted world, woven with dreams.

Petals unfurl, their colors blend,
A symphony of shades so rare,
Each moment a stroke on nature's brush,
A tapestry spun with tender care.

In the garden, laughter sings,
Children chase where the blooms sway,
Each bud a promise, each leaf a tale,
Of fleeting hours in bright array.

As daylight fades, the canvas glows,
Stars punctuate the velvet night,
In this soft world, we find our peace,
Amidst the embrace of evening light.

When the World Turns to Frost

With a hush, the cold winds sigh,
White blankets cover the earth below,
Frozen whispers fill the air,
As twilight casts a silvery glow.

Footsteps crunch on snow-kissed ground,
A delicate dance of silence unfolds,
Each breath visible, crisp and clear,
The charm of winter, a tale retold.

Branches wear their icy crowns,
Nature's artistry, pure and stark,
The world transformed, soft and bright,
Magic lingers in the dark.

Underneath the frozen sky,
Hearts gather close, wrapped in dreams,
In the cold, warmth comes alive,
With gentle light from flickering beams.

Ribbons of Ice and Dreams

Moonlight glimmers on icy streams,
Ribbons of silver, soft and bright,
Whispered secrets in the night air,
Reflecting stars, pure delight.

Trees adorned with crystal lace,
Each branch a pearl, each twig a gem,
Nature's treasures, wondrous grace,
In winter's embrace, life feels like a dream.

Footsteps echo through the still,
A journey crafted in frosty hues,
With every step, the earth breathes slow,
A dance of ice, of sighs, and muse.

As dawn arrives, the world sleeps on,
Wrapped in the quiet, serene glow,
In this realm, where dreams take flight,
Hearts find solace, and spirits grow.

The Quietude of Winter's Lullaby

Gently falling, the snow descends,
A soft blanket on the world so wide,
Each flake a whisper, soft and light,
Winter's lullaby, a tender guide.

The air is still, a breath is caught,
Silence weaves its gentle thread,
Wrapped in warmth, we find our peace,
In the hush, where dreams are fed.

Stars twinkle down from heavens high,
As the moon cradles the sleeping earth,
In this calm, hearts intertwine,
Finding joy in the season's mirth.

When morning dawns, the world will wake,
But for now, let the silence stay,
In winter's arms, we find our rest,
In the quietude, where hopes softly play.

Echoes of Silence in the Cold

Whispers dance in the frozen night,
Stars twinkle with a gentle light.
Footsteps crunch on the brittle ground,
In stillness, lost secrets abound.

Reflections mirror the pale moon,
Lonesome night sings a haunting tune.
Each breath visible, a fleeting mist,
In silence, we find what we've missed.

Shadows stretch beneath ancient trees,
Time pauses in the chill of the breeze.
Frosted edges, a quiet embrace,
Echoes linger in this lonely space.

Memories drift with the falling snow,
In each silence, deeper truths flow.
The cold grips tight, yet hearts will warm,
In shadows cast by winter's charm.

The Stillness of Breath in Snow-Laden Air

Snowflakes settle on weary ground,
Each soft flake is a whispered sound.
Quietness blankets the worn-out lane,
In this stillness, we ease the pain.

Breathe in deep of the crisp, pure air,
Traces of warmth linger everywhere.
In moments where the world stands still,
Time slows down, obeying our will.

Branches bow with a weight so bright,
Glistening softly in pale moonlight.
Every breath feels like a gentle sigh,
In winter's hush, our spirits fly.

The air is thick with dreams and peace,
In the stillness, our thoughts cease.
Snow-laden moments, pure and rare,
Craft memories in the silent air.

Winter's Embrace

Cloaked in white, the world turns serene,
In winter's arms, all feels unseen.
Gentle breezes kiss frosted pines,
Nature whispers through tangled vines.

The sun, a shy guest in the sky,
Paints the horizon with a soft sigh.
Fires crackle with warmth and cheer,
While silence cradles all we hold dear.

Frozen lakes reflect silver dreams,
In their depths, the cold moon beams.
Creatures burrow, snug and tight,
While the world rests in frosted night.

With each breath, a moment to cherish,
In winter's touch, our worries perish.
Embrace the chill, let go of haste,
In the still of winter, life is graced.

The Warmth of Frosted Dreams

Tender visions in crystal light,
Glowing softly in the deep of night.
Frosted moments dance in the air,
While whispers tell tales beyond compare.

Each twinkle sparkles like lost hope,
In a world where we dare to cope.
Dreams unfurl in the hush of snow,
As warmth ignites with a gentle glow.

Under blankets of white, we lie,
Tracing patterns as stars occupy.
In every flake, a story woven,
Where fables of love to warmth are driven.

The heart beats strong, though cold surrounds,
In frosted dreams, our joy abounds.
Let winter's chill foster inner fire,
For in these dreams, we will aspire.

Nights Adrift in a Crystal Sea

Beneath a sky of endless dreams,
The stars like jewels brightly gleam.
Soft waves whisper in the night,
A dance of shadows, a gentle flight.

The moon reflects on waters deep,
Where secrets of the ocean sleep.
With every breeze, a story flows,
Of distant shores, the heart knows.

In silence, time begins to weave,
A tapestry of dusk and eve.
The horizon melts into the dark,
A canvas painted with a spark.

Adrift in thoughts, the soul shall roam,
In this crystal sea, I find my home.
The night, a lullaby so sweet,
Echoes softly through my heartbeat.

The Gentle Caress of Icy Breezes

Through winter's breath, the cold winds sigh,
They kiss the earth and drift on by.
A soft embrace, so pure and clear,
Inviting whispers, drawing near.

The world is draped in shades of white,
As frozen branches catch the light.
Each crystal spark a fleeting glance,
Nature's tranquil, snowy dance.

Beneath the boughs, the silence grows,
In every flake, a secret glows.
Wrapped in warmth, the heart ignites,
With joyful dreams on chilly nights.

Icy breezes weave through the trees,
A gentle touch, an evening tease.
In the stillness, true peace we find,
In nature's grip, our hearts unwind.

A Symphony of Snow and Solitude

Silent flurries begin to fall,
A white embrace, a quiet call.
Each flake a note in winter's song,
As solitude plays all night long.

The world is hushed, a peaceful dome,
Covered paths lead us back home.
With every breath, the cold air stings,
Yet warms the heart, as nature sings.

In solitude, our thoughts take flight,
With dreams alight in the pale moonlight.
Snowflakes drift like notes on air,
A symphonic dance, beyond compare.

As midnight falls, the world transforms,
In this cold embrace, the spirit warms.
Together, snow and silence blend,
A beautiful journey that will not end.

Moonlit Whispers in the Frosted Air

In the hush of night, the moonlight glows,
Casting shadows where no one goes.
Whispers dance on frosted breath,
A tale of life, a kiss of death.

Stars twinkle softly, a guiding light,
Marking paths throughout the night.
The chill surrounds, yet hearts stay warm,
Held by dreams, away from harm.

Each step a crunch, a whispered sound,
On this sacred, frozen ground.
The night unfolds its silver thread,
In moonlit whispers, all is said.

With every glance, the world reveals,
The beauty in what darkness conceals.
Under the gaze of celestial grace,
We find ourselves in this silent space.

The Comfort of Snowflakes and Stillness

Softly they fall, a gentle dance,
Whispering peace in their silent prance.
Each flake a quilt, a tender embrace,
Wrapping the world in a quiet place.

Stars twinkle bright, in the deep night sky,
Snowflakes reflect, with their silent sigh.
Nature's soft breath, in a winter's chill,
Brings comfort and warmth, a soul's gentle thrill.

Hearthside Reflections in the Chill

Flickering flames in the fireplace glow,
While icy winds around the house blow.
Memories dance like the shadows cast,
Moments we cherish, that forever last.

Wrapped in a blanket, we share our tales,
Hot cocoa warms as the cold wind wails.
Laughter and love fill the evening air,
In the hearthside glow, we find our care.

Enchanted by the Winter Night

Moonlight glistens on the snow below,
As the world shimmers with a silver glow.
Frosted trees stand in majestic grace,
Whispers of magic in this tranquil space.

Footsteps crunch softly, breaking the peace,
In the heart of winter, all worries cease.
Night's gentle embrace, a dreamlike sight,
We are enchanted by the winter night.

Cradled in the Arms of Frost

The world is hushed beneath the white sheet,
Where everything sparkles in the cold meet.
Nature's pure canvas, untouched and bright,
Cradles our hearts in the still of the night.

The breath of winter kisses our skin,
In the frosty air, new dreams begin.
Embraced by the quiet, we find our way,
Cradled in frost, we embrace the day.

Chilling Elegance Beneath the Stars

In twilight's glow, the night awakes,
The silver stars in silence blink.
Moonlight dances on crisp lakes,
As whispers weave where shadows sink.

A chill wraps round the sleeping earth,
Each breath a cloud, a dream anew.
Nature sighs with quiet mirth,
In elegance, the dark imbues.

Trees adorned in icy lace,
Stand tall against the winter's might.
In this realm, we find our place,
Where beauty thrives in silver light.

Here, hearts flutter in stillness deep,
Underneath the vast expanse.
The night, its secrets ours to keep,
A chilling elegance, a trance.

Comfort Found in the Cold

Frosty fingers tap at panes,
Breath visible in morning's light.
Each flake whispers of gentle rains,
In winter's grasp, all feels right.

Warmth of layers, snug and tight,
The world transformed, soft and white.
Sipping cocoa by the fire,
Comfort blooms as dreams aspire.

Snowflakes twirl like soft ballet,
In quiet grace, they drift and sway.
A cozy hug, the heart's embrace,
In chilly air, I find my place.

Nature rests, a quiet sleep,
While we in warmth and joy do keep.
In icy breaths, a joy unfolds,
Discovering comfort in the cold.

A Retreat from the Winter's Wrath

Outside, the winds fiercely blow,
But inside glows a warm retreat.
Footsteps crunch on fresh, white snow,
In comfort's grip, we find our seat.

Fires crackle, stories shared,
Laughter dances in the air.
In this haven, hearts are bared,
Against the storm, we show we care.

The world beyond, a tempest wild,
Yet here, all is calm and serene.
With every warmth, like a child,
In blissful joy, we reign supreme.

Let the snowflakes spin and whirl,
We'll journey deep into our dreams.
In this retreat, our spirits twirl,
Against winter's wrath, hope redeems.

Enchanted by the Frosty Glow

Enchantment glows in winter's night,
Where breath turns clouds in silver streams.
Frosty jewels in soft moonlight,
Kiss the earth with sparkles and gleams.

Each crystal flake a whispered tale,
A frosty breath in swirling flight.
The air is crisp, the stars unveil,
A magic dance of sheer delight.

Shadows twist beneath the pines,
As whispers weave through bitter cold.
In nature's calm, the heart aligns,
To find its joy, a warmth untold.

Together in this wondrous glow,
Our souls ignited by the night.
In winter's arms, love starts to grow,
Enchanted by the frost, so bright.

Pillows of Snow

Softly they fall, a gentle sigh,
Blanketing earth, as time slips by.
Whispers of winter, peaceful and bright,
Cradled in silence, wrapped in white.

Children laugh, their joy released,
Building memories, a winter feast.
Snowflakes dance in the crisp night air,
Each one unique, a treasure rare.

Night descends, stars shine above,
A quiet world, a story of love.
Pillows of snow, soft and profound,
Nature's embrace, serenity found.

Dreams Afloat

Drifting on clouds, where wishes are born,
Gentle whispers of hope, in the morn.
Laughter and light, sharing the sky,
Dreams afloat, a heart learning to fly.

Each passing moment, a treasure to hold,
Stories of wonder, in silence unfold.
Wings of the spirit, so freely we chase,
Floating on dreams, in a boundless space.

The world below, a distant ballet,
Embracing the magic, we float away.
In shadows of night, our hopes take flight,
Together we'll wander, into the light.

The Gentle Caress of Cold

In the stillness, a breath of frost,
Nature's whispers, a line uncrossed.
A gentle caress, the earth in repose,
Winter's soft touch, where tranquility grows.

Trees stand tall, clad in icy lace,
Embracing the chill, they find their grace.
Frost-kissed mornings, sparkling and bright,
Each moment cherished, a pure delight.

Crystals shimmer in the pale moonlight,
Sorrows vanish, troubles take flight.
In the embrace of the winter's hold,
We find a warmth in the stories told.

Serenity Found in Flurries

Flurries descend, a soft ballet,
Transforming the world in a tender display.
Tiny white dancers, swirling with glee,
Bringing a stillness, setting us free.

In the chaos, a moment of peace,
Nature's beauty grants sweet release.
Each flake a blessing, floating down slow,
A reminder of love in the gentle glow.

Footprints imprinted on shimmering ground,
Marking a journey where joy can be found.
Serenity whispers in the silent night,
Wrapped in the wonder of winter's light.

Illuminated by Winter's Light

Softly it glows, the pale winter sun,
Lighting the way for all to run.
Frosted branches catch a glimmering gleam,
Illuminated beauty, a fleeting dream.

Days grow short, but hearts feel alive,
In the chill of the air, we thrive.
Every twinkle of ice, a promise anew,
Winter's embrace, a canvas so true.

The world, a wonder, bathed in white,
Every corner bright, every shadow light.
In the stillness, magic takes flight,
Unified souls in winter's soft light.

Warmth in the Winter's Tale

In the hearth's glow, shadows dance,
Flickering flames, a warm romance.
Snow falls gently, a soft embrace,
Hearts aglow in this frosty space.

Laughter echoes through the night,
Bundled close, we feel the light.
Outside the chill, inside we sigh,
Together, love will always fly.

Kisses from the Frozen Horizon

The sun dips low, a golden blaze,
Kisses from dusk, a warming phase.
Frosted branches, a sparkling view,
Whispers of love in the evening dew.

Paths unwind through a snowy drift,
Winter's breath, a tender gift.
Every step, a soft caress,
In this quiet, we find our rest.

The Night's Shimmering Veil

Stars collected in a velvet dome,
Each a story, each a home.
The moon spills light on fields so pale,
Wrapping the world in a shimmering veil.

Silence reigns under a frosty night,
Magic settles, a peaceful sight.
In this calm, our dreams take flight,
Wrapped in wonder, held so tight.

Chasing Snowflakes

Dancing through the frosty air,
Snowflakes flutter everywhere.
Children laugh, their joy set free,
In this moment, pure ecstasy.

Each flake a wish, each twirl a dream,
The world is glowing, a silver gleam.
We chase the wonders, hearts so light,
In winter's grip, everything feels right.

Finding Peace

In the stillness of the snowy night,
A peaceful heart can find the light.
Beneath the stars, the world feels whole,
Winter whispers to the soul.

Hot cocoa warms our chilled fingertips,
Fireside dreams on lingering sips.
Here we gather, stories to share,
In this moment, love's rich air.

Chasing Shadows in the Snowfall

Footprints dance on velvet white,
Whispers echo in the night.
Children laughing, hearts aglow,
Chasing shadows in the snow.

Moonlight glimmers, stars ignite,
Every flake a soft delight.
In this world of cold and glow,
We find joy as we bestow.

Winds will carry winter's call,
Through the silence, we enthrall.
Joy and laughter, warm and slow,
Chasing shadows in the snow.

As the dawn begins to break,
Nature stirs from slumber's sake.
With the sun, our spirits grow,
In this chase, our hearts do flow.

A Lunchtime Lullaby Under Frozen Skies

Underneath the boughs so deep,
Nature sings a tune to keep.
With each bite, the chill seems fade,
A warm embrace in snow's cascade.

Children gather, eyes alight,
Sharing stories, pure delight.
Underneath those frozen skies,
Laughter rings, and spirits rise.

Time stands still in frosty air,
Each moment beyond compare.
With our breath, we paint the day,
A lullaby in winter's play.

As the clouds drift gently past,
In this haven, we are cast.
Every heartbeat sings the tune,
Magic found beneath the moon.

Twilight Tales of Snow and Serenity

As twilight falls, the world transforms,
Blankets of snow in gentle swarms.
Whispers of stillness fill the air,
In this peace, we cease to care.

Shadows stretch, the silence deep,
While the stars begin to peep.
In this moment, time stands still,
With every breath, we feel the chill.

Tales are told in muted tones,
Wrapped in warmth, where love condones.
The wonder of a world so bright,
Twilight dances, pure delight.

With every flake that drifts and swirls,
We find beauty in the pearls.
Snowflakes falling, soft and free,
In their descent, pure serenity.

Quiet Moments Beneath Glistening Branches

Beneath the branches, glistening bright,
We find solace in soft light.
Snowy whispers brush our skin,
Quiet moments, peace within.

Nature holds its breath to see,
In the stillness, we can be.
Every flake a gentle embrace,
In this haven, we find grace.

Branches bow with frosty weight,
We sit and ponder, contemplate.
With each breath, the world slows down,
In this wonderland, we drown.

As the day fades into night,
Stars awaken, sparkling bright.
Quiet moments, hearts aligned,
In this beauty, peace we find.

Beneath a Blanket of White

Snowflakes dance in the cold air,
Whispers of winter everywhere.
Covering earth with soft grace,
Nature's quilt, a pure embrace.

Footsteps crunch on the fresh ground,
Silence reigns, a peaceful sound.
Trees adorned in frosty lace,
Beneath a blanket, time's slow pace.

Children laugh in pure delight,
Building dreams in the twilight.
Snowmen rise, bright faces beam,
Beneath the stars, a cozy dream.

The night descends, the world sleeps tight,
Wrapped in fluff, a soft white light.
Under moons that softly gleam,
Winter whispers, a gentle dream.

Stars Weave Through the Chill

In the still of the night sky,
Stars sparkle, twinkling high.
Winter's breath, crisp and clear,
Weaving magic, drawing near.

Each glittering light, a story told,
Of nights cloaked in blankets cold.
The moon hangs low, a watchful gaze,
Guiding hearts through frosty haze.

Underneath the brilliant glow,
Chill winds whisper secrets slow.
Dreams take flight, on frosty wings,
As the winter night softly sings.

Time feels still, the world at peace,
In this silence, worries cease.
Stars weave tales, both near and far,
In the chill, each heart's a star.

The Hushed Whispers of Winter

Gentle flakes fall, soft as sighs,
Winter's breath in quiet skies.
Each flake tells a tale of old,
In whispers sweet, the night unfolds.

The world is wrapped in a frosted hush,
As nature pauses, time turns to mush.
Branches bow with a silver crown,
In winter's magic, we won't drown.

Footprints trace a story rare,
In the stillness, we share a prayer.
Candlelight flickers, warmth inside,
As winter wraps us, like a guide.

Here in the silence, hearts ignite,
In the shadows, love feels right.
The hushed whispers call us near,
In winter's arms, we hold no fear.

Embracing the Icy Silence

Frosted windows, a world confined,
In icy silence, peace we find.
Softly falling, the world transforms,
Winter's embrace in quiet forms.

The air is sharp, yet calm prevails,
As nature writes its timeless tales.
Wrapped in layers, we breathe in slow,
Embracing the chill, letting warmth flow.

Each breath forms a cloud in the night,
In the stillness, everything feels right.
The heart beats slow, in rhythmic time,
In the cosmos, nature's rhyme.

The icy silence holds a song,
A melody where we belong.
Together we stand, a moment so bright,
In winter's arms, we find our light.

When the World Pauses to Dream

In twilight's soft embrace, we sigh,
As stars peek down from the sky.
Whispers of hope begin to scheme,
When the world pauses to dream.

The moon casts silver on the ground,
Nature's hush, a soothing sound.
In this moment, hearts do gleam,
When the world pauses to dream.

With every breath, a wish takes flight,
Through velvet shadows cloaked in night.
Unraveling thoughts, a gentle stream,
When the world pauses to dream.

Time stands still, in wonder's sway,
As night gives way to dawning day.
In slumber's arms, we softly beam,
When the world pauses to dream.

Flurries and Flickers in Harmony

Snowflakes dance upon the breeze,
Flickers of warmth, like whispers tease.
In the stillness, a beauty found,
Flurries and flickers spin around.

Candles glow in windows bright,
Casting shadows soft and light.
A symphony of cold and fire,
Flurries and flickers lift us higher.

Outside, a world draped white and pure,
Inside, we gather, hearts secure.
Through the chill, love we surround,
Flurries and flickers spin around.

In this dance, we find our place,
A gentle warmth, a sweet embrace.
Together we stand, joyous and proud,
Flurries and flickers, laugh loud.

A Canvas of Peace Beneath Boughs

Under branches, shadows play,
Where soft whispers guide the way.
Nature's palette, calm and bright,
A canvas of peace, pure delight.

Rustling leaves tell tales of old,
Crickets serenade, their songs bold.
In this haven, time flows slow,
A canvas of peace, in nature's glow.

Sunlight spills through gaps so fine,
Dancing winds, a gentle line.
In the quiet, our spirits grow,
A canvas of peace, where dreams flow.

Each heartbeat echoes nature's rhyme,
Moments captured, lost in time.
Beneath boughs' grace, we come to know,
A canvas of peace, love's soft glow.

Hushed Reveries on a Winter's Eve

In the stillness, shadows creep,
While the world around us sleeps.
Hushed reveries, soft and brief,
On a winter's eve, we seek relief.

Frosted windows, patterns bold,
Stories of warmth, softly told.
Cocoa steam swirls, a gentle weave,
In hushed reveries on a winter's eve.

Embers crackle, glow and fade,
Wrapped in blankets, dreams are made.
With each sigh, our hearts believe,
In hushed reveries on a winter's eve.

Snowflakes twinkle like hopes anew,
The night, a canvas set for two.
In quiet moments, we find reprieve,
In hushed reveries on a winter's eve.